MISSING IN ACTION

SEVENTY-TWO DAYS BEHIND ENEMY LINES
1945

BILL PETTY

Copyright © 1990. John William Petty.
All rights reserved.
ISBN: 979-8-296-05591-0

Second Printing: August 2025

Dedicated to my wife, Geraldine, who lived every moment of this experience with me. She never gave up and never stopped praying that I would return. Also, to my children and grandchildren for insisting that I put the "behind enemy lines" experiences in a book that could be passed on to their children.

INTRODUCTION

Too often when we read chronicles of American history, we read about faceless people in faraway places. And, although we are taught the significance of the battles and the treaties, we fail to personally connect with the men and women who have so valiantly served our country. *Missing in Action*, Bill Petty's account of the 72 days he spent in enemy territory breaks that mold as it passionately describes his odyssey in Yugoslavia. Petty also details searching for and eventually finding the woman who saved him and his crew from capture and then led them to safety.

During World War II, Smith County resident Bill Petty served in the Air Force as nose-gunner on a B-24 bomber. I commend his bravery and skill. Our nation needs more people like Bill Petty—people who serve their country with determination and courage and then share their experiences with future generations. Fans of American history and Tennesseans of all ages owe a debt of gratitude to Bill Petty for *Missing in Action*.

Albert Gore Jr.
United States Senator
State of Tennessee

FOREWORD

I am honored to write words of introduction to Bill Petty's heroic saga of an incident that occurred during World War II. Bill's story and thousands of similar stories, most of them untold, of gallant action and individual determination are some of the facets that made the Army Air Forces such a formidable force during World War II and provided a wonderful tradition for the United States Air Force that would follow in the ensuing years.

Today, many Americans do not know of the resistance to the Axis Powers by patriotic men and women in all countries that were overrun by the Germans, Italians, and Japanese. Much has been written, and rightly so, about the French resistance fighters and the guerrilla fighters in the Philippines, for instance. Not so much has been written or is known about the Yugoslavian resistance, initially the Royalist fighters, the Chetniks, under General Mihailovic, and the partisan forces of Tito, a Communist, with this internal struggle eventually being won by Tito's forces. These resistance fighters are the ones without whose assistance Bill Petty and many other Allied airmen would not have been returned to the control of our own forces. A great debt of gratitude is owed to all those partisans, guerrillas, and resistance fighters who struggled behind enemy lines, many times with hope as their only beacon.

I served as Director of the United States Air Force Museum at Wright-Patterson AFB, Ohio from 1970 to 1976. Our mission there was to tell and present the story of the United States Air Force and its predecessor organizations to the visiting public. That story is one of which all Americans can be proud. Bill Petty's story told in this book is a vital part of the larger history of the United States Air Force. We are all indebted to him for writing it for posterity.

Bernie S. Bass, *Colonel USAF (Ret)*

ACKNOWLEDGEMENTS

A special thanks too . . .

Bernie S. Bass for writing the forward to this book. Colonel Bass was a distinguished P-40 and P-47 fighter-bomber pilot during World War II.

Janko Kranjc and Bogomil Hvala, the first Partisans we contacted. They set us on a course that led to freedom 72 days later.

Darko Ohojak who rescued our co-pilot Lt. Trebusak and our gunner Sgt. Baumgardner, along with thanks to his son Davor Ohojak.

The many people in Yugoslavia who helped me and the other crew members shot down behind enemy lines.

Senator Albert Gore, Jr., for his kind endorsement.

Edi Šelhaus, for permitting me to use photos from his book *Fotoreporter* and for arranging for a perfect day of visiting with our helpers in 1976.

The Faletič family, who hid me, along with two other crew members, five days and nights while the Germans searched the hills for us. Mrs. Faletič was 88 years old when I returned to her home in 1969. She died at age 95.

Andrej Pagon Ogarev, reporter, who covered our return to Yugoslavia in 1976, along with Edi Šelhaus, writer and photographer.

Brave pilots who landed behind enemy lines to bring us to safety.

Jerry Armstrong, pilot, who stayed with the falling bomber until all crew members had exited.

My Heavenly Father, who answered the prayers of my wife, friends, and family. My wife wrote to me daily, even though she knew there was no mail call behind enemy lines.

Sergeant John William Petty, United States Air Force

This book is not about bravery and heroism. I am one of the fortunate survivors. I have written some of the incidents and mysteries that occurred behind the lines as I recall them. They are stamped in my mind, never to be forgotten.

The real heroes were the brave men from all branches of the military service who gave their lives for their country. Their wives, children, fathers, and mothers had to carry on with the hope that they would again see their loved ones in the Great Beyond. My gratitude and prayers go out to them for making the supreme gift of a loved one. They gave their lives that you and I might have freedom in the greatest nation on Earth.

BASIC TRAINING

On November 10, 1942, I left my home at Carthage, Tennessee, traveling to Nashville, a distance of about fifty miles, to volunteer to serve in the Army Air Force. I was sworn into service the following day and was assigned to an Air Force Training Base at Macon, Georgia. I had been married only a few months, and my wife, Geraldine, and I thought it best for me to volunteer rather than wait to be drafted. Induction left no choice of branch of service.

Geraldine spent a part of the first year of my service with me, in rooms with the Carter family. This family, with their daughter, Becky, cared for her as if she were their own. Soon we were expecting our first child. All thought it best for her to return home to be near her parents.

My work as a mechanic was on BT-13A (training) planes. After almost one year's service, I volunteered to fly, hoping to become a pilot in the Air Force. I made application, passed the tests, and was sent to Miami, Florida for further testing.

Geraldine, my wife, and Rebecca Carter Cassidy

On December 2, 1943, Janice Gaye was born into our family. She was a beautiful, healthy baby, and we had much for which to be thankful. I received an emergency call from the Red Cross to come home at that time. I came home to see my wife and new daughter. I then returned to Miami to continue the exams and tests for pilot training.

Bill Petty in cockpit of trainer

One of the low points of my Army service came when I was told that instead of pilot training I would be sent to gunnery school to become an aerial gunner. I never received an explanation of why

Bill Petty and crew members

On leave in Georgia

I was changed, only that the Air Force needed gunners more than pilots.

After a sad Christmas in Miami, I was shipped to Harlingen Air Force Base, Harlingen, Texas, for aerial gunnery training. If this was to be my lot, I would accept it. About ninety percent of volunteers for pilot training met with the same fate. The testing center did let some personnel return to their former branch of service.

Our gunnery training was very thorough. It was three months of learning all about 50-caliber machine guns, how to shoot at moving targets, both from the air and the sea (the Gulf of Mexico) and on land. We learned to shoot from the back of pickup trucks with 12-gauge shotguns at moving targets on a trap and skeet range. We shot at targets placed on small boats in the Gulf of Mexico and at targets towed by planes. We were able to take a machine gun apart and reassemble it blindfolded before graduation day.

From Harlingen, Texas, I was sent to Lincoln, Nebraska, an assembly base for Air Force crews, and en route I spent a few days at home. We stayed in Lincoln only long enough for personnel to be assigned to planes. We were assigned to a B-24 Liberator bomber and then proceeded to Casper, Wyoming, for final training. The ten men for our plane consisted of pilot, Lt. Gerald S. Armstrong, Maple Heights, Ohio; co-pilot, Lt. Frank Trebusak, LaSalle, Illinois; navigator, Lt. William Hockensmith, Lexington, Kentucky; bombardier, Lt. Ballard Cooper, Pocatello, Idaho; engineer, Sgt. Leo J. Lord, Fitchburg, Massachusetts; assistant engineer and nose gunner, John W. Petty, Carthage, Tennessee; radio operator, Thaddeus M. Witkowski, Chicago, Illinois; ball turret gunner, Clinton K. Mitchell, Enid, Oklahoma; waist gunner, Jay Wilson, Hyrum, Utah; tail gunner, Duane M. Mascik, Conneaut, Ohio.

Front row: Lt. Gerald Armstrong, pilot; Lt. Frank Trebusak, co-pilot; Lt. Bill Hockensmith, navigator; Lt. Ballard Cooper, bombardier.
Back row: Sgt. Duane Mascik, tail gunner; Sgt. Frank Mitchell, ball turret gunner; Sgt. Leo Lord, engineer; Sgt. Bill Petty, nose gunner and asst. engineer; Sgt. Ted Witkowski, radio operator; Sgt. Jay Wilson, gunner.

211th Army Air Force Base Unit (CCTS) (H)
Army Air Field
Casper, Wyoming

This is to Certify, That _____

CORPORAL JOHN W PETTY

has satisfactorily completed the course
of training for combat crews
as prescribed by Headquarters, Second Air Force
and given at
Army Air Field, Casper, Wyoming

Given on this ___TWENTY-NINTH___ day of ___JULY___
in the year of Our Lord, one thousand, nine hundred and forty=four.

Attest:

McLyle G. Zumwalt
Director of Training

McLyle G. Zumwalt
Major, Air Corps

E. M. Hampton
Commanding

E. M. Hampton
Colonel, Air Corps

Certificate of training

Our crew was assigned to the air base at Casper, Wyoming. There we would train as a crew on a B-24 bomber, under the leadership of our pilot, Jerry Armstrong, a Christian gentleman and outstanding pilot.

Many of the wives, girlfriends, and family members of our crew came to visit with us for a short time. This would be our final chance to be close to our loved ones before going into combat.

Geraldine came with Gaye, our eight-month-old daughter, who was our pride and joy. This was both a happy and a sad time. We were together, but we knew we would soon be separated. Many tears were shed as separation time came. We were then shipped to Camp Kilmer, New Jersey, for transport to the combat area.

We left New York on August 10, 1944, on the troop ship, Alexandria. We watched the Statue of Liberty disappear as we sailed out to sea. Leaving my country was a strange feeling, one which I had never experienced before. We were part of a huge convoy of ships with destroyers to protect us from submarine attacks. We crossed the Atlantic and landed in Liverpool, England, on August 24, 1944.

We left England and were assigned to the 15th Air Force in Italy. Leaving on September 4, we went to Casablanca and continued on

Our base at Spinazzola

to Naples, Italy, on September 6. On September 8, our assignment to the 460th Bombardment Group, 761 Squadron in Spinazzola, Italy, came from headquarters in Bari, Italy.

After flying a few more training missions, we were scheduled to fly our first combat mission. I have to say that we were apprehensive about what to expect and were told by some of the veteran crews to expect the worst. This caused the powdered eggs for breakfast to go down in a lump. We made the first mission and soon had the jaunty air of veterans. Over the next four months, we flew a total of seventeen missions—the dates, locations, and times as follows:

1. September 17, Budapest, Hungary – Oil Refineries,
   Time: 6 hrs. 45 min.
2. September 20, Hatvan, Hungary – Railroad Yards,
   Time: 7 hrs. 45 min.
3. September 23, Casarsa, North Italy – R.R. Bridge,
   Time: 6 hrs. 05 min.
4. September 24, Salonika, Greece – Troop Excavating Boats,
   Time: 5 hrs. 45 min.
5. October 4, Avisio, Italy – Railroad Viaduct,
   Time: 7 hrs. 20 min.
6. October 7, Vienna, Austria – Oil Storage Tanks,
   Time: 7 hrs. 0 min.
7. October 10, Piave, Susegana, North Italy – Bridge,
   Time: 6 hrs. 10 min.
8. October 20, Rosenheim, Austria – R. R. Marshaling Yards,
   Time: 7 hrs. 25 min.
9. October 23, Augsburg, Germany – Mfg. Factories,
   Time: 8hrs. 45 min.
10. November 4, Linz, Austria – Oil Refineries,
    Time: 7 hrs. 45 min.
11. November 6, Vienna, Austria – Ordinance Dept.,
    Time: 6 hrs. 40 min.
12. November 7, Mezzocorona, Italy – R. R. Bridge,
    Time: 7 hrs. 0 min.

13. November 16, Prispolje, Yugoslavia – Troop Movements,
    Time: 4 hrs. 25 min.
14. November 18, Udine, Italy – Airfields,
    Time: 5 hrs. 40 min.
15. December 2, Blechhammer, Germany – Oil Refineries,
    Time: 8 hrs. 20 min.
16. December 28, Prague, Czechoslovakia – Kralupy Oil Field,
    Time: 8 hrs. 0 min.
17. January 20, Linz, Austria – Bombed Alt. Target, Rosenheim, Austria; our plane goes down.

The record of these missions was kept in a diary on a small note pad, along with flight time, location, targets, escort planes, amount of flack encountered, and name of the plane we flew. The log of our missions continued only through the seventeenth. The last mission led to one of the greatest adventures of my life.

Heavy flak over enemy target

Smoke rising from bombed targets in Graz, Austria

THE FATEFUL MISSION

On January 20, 1945, a B-24 Liberator bomber of the 761st Squadron, 460th Bombardment Group set out from its base at Spinazzola, Italy on an ordinary mission to bomb German positions at Linz, Austria. I was nose gunner and assistant engineer aboard that bomber. After sixteen missions, I had little reason to suspect that this mission would be my last.

Our bomber – "Dinah-Might"

We had been briefed by our intelligence officers to expect Linz to be well fortified, since anti-aircraft fire from the ground had been intense on previous missions. As we approached the target, the view from my nose-gun position was almost too good. The greeting we got was not pleasant. It seemed as if they were all set for our heading. The sky seemed to be black with shells bursting in the air.

The anti-aircraft shells filled with high explosives could bring a plane down with one direct hit, and they were timed to explode at a certain altitude. Our escorts were P-51 fighter planes flown by the only black group of fighter pilots in the Air Force, the 99th Fighter Group. We felt good knowing that they were there to keep enemy planes from attacking us.

Bill Petty on nose-gun position (Janice Gaye, his daughter's name painted below turret)

On our final approach to the target, something happened to our squadron's lead plane. It veered away from the target, followed by all seven planes in our squadron. The message came that we were to bomb the alternate target—Rosenheim, Austria. The target would be railroad cars filled with war material. In a very short time, we would drop our bombs on the target and head for our home base. Taking a heading across the Alps, we would soon reach the Adriatic Sea, then fly south to our base in southern Italy. Little did we know that we would never complete our mission.

As I looked to the right, I could see other planes which had already dropped their bombs approaching the coastline near Udine, Italy. In a matter of minutes, we would be over the Adriatic Sea and out of danger of anti-aircraft fire. This was not to be. One of our engines started racing wildly and then almost quit. This was followed by the other three engines. Too late we discovered that our gas tanks were running on empty. We began to lose power; Leo Lord, our engineer, quickly started transferring the small amount of gas left in the auxiliary tanks. There were only 150 gallons in each wingtip, and all but a small, precious amount had already been transferred to our main tanks about an hour after leaving our base that morning. Pilot Jerry Armstrong and co-pilot Trebusak quickly made a 180-degree turn as we lost altitude; we would try to get back into the Alps Mountains before bailing out. We had been briefed by our intelligence officer that underground Partisans would be in certain locations in the mountains. We hoped to be rescued before being captured.

The reason for our lack of fuel is something of a mystery. First, our regular plane, Dinah-Might, had been grounded for inspection during this mission. We were flying another crew's plane, called Slick-Chick-with-a-Hot-Lick. Our crew had always performed their duties well. I am uncertain about the condition of the plane we used that day. Perhaps it used more fuel. Also, since we were in heavy flack, we may have taken a hit in our fuel
tank. I only know that the fuel for the flight was not sufficient.

On our way to the mountains, we passed over Udine, Italy. The bombardier bailed out in the heavy flack and—we learned later—was captured. I feel sure he thought the plane might go out of control at any minute, and he did not wait for orders. By now the other planes from our squadron had continued their course home. It was a sad feeling to be left behind.

A fighter pilot in one of the P-51s zoomed by to let us know he was staying with us to keep enemy fighters from finishing us off.

The fighter pilot had very little fuel in his own tanks and would not be able to get back to the base if he did not leave at once. He dipped the plane's wings in saying goodbye and to let us know that we had not "gone down" to our fate unnoticed. We were very grateful to a brave pilot who did not want to leave us alone. We now had to face the grim reality of our situation. In only a few more precious minutes, this plane would crash in the rugged mountains. All four engines were cutting off and on for lack of sufficient fuel.

Our plane was losing altitude fast, and the order to bail out was given. Quickly backing out of my nose turret—no time to grab my camera stored nearby, I stuffed my canteen of frozen water in my pocket and tied a pair of G.I. shoes to my parachute harness. The oxygen mask was still on my face as I disconnected the hose and intercom.

My bailout exit was a small door where the nose wheel retracted. I pulled the handle that would release the door, but the door was stuck and would not budge. I did not waste any time. I crawled under the flight deck and jumped through the open bomb bay doors. I was thankful to get out of the plane safely, but I found myself tumbling through space at a blinding speed. This type of jump does not occur in training. No rip cord is pulled automatically, and you are on your own. I thought there must be a way to stop this tumbling. I threw my arms straight out. This left me falling feet down with my arms high in the air, pulled there by the force of the fall. I gradually lowered my arms and grasped the parachute harness. I knew I had delayed the opening long enough. Grabbing the rip cord, I gave it a quick pull. The parachute opened with a big jerk that ripped my shoes off, and my oxygen mask ended up on top of my head. Floating in space, I thanked God that my chute had opened.

I looked to the left and saw two chutes open, and to my right I could see two more of my friends floating toward earth. These two were Leo Lord, engineer, and J. W. Brock, tailgunner. Brock broke his leg when he had a rough landing. I looked down to find the earth coming up to me very quickly. I pulled one shroud line of the chute to avoid a big tree, but it was too late. I fell through the branches. The tree broke my fall.

I was lucky that my chute hung high in a tree, with my feet barely touching the earth, for it gave me a soft landing. The snow was between two and three feet deep. Rifle shots were too close for comfort. I looked in the snow to see if the bullets were hitting near me. Then I unbuckled my chute harness and left the chute hanging in the tree. I knew the enemy must have captured Leo and Brock since they came down in the small town. I was on the edge of town with the Alps Mountains rising high on each side. When I looked at my watch, I found it was 2 p.m., Saturday, January 20. I must get into the mountain fast, if I was to evade capture. It seemed I was moving up the mountain five or ten feet at a time, sometimes sliding back more than I gained. Soon I heard a noise coming from the mountain. It was Ted Witkowski and Elmo Justilian, our radio operator and camera man. They were going into town to seek refuge with a priest. Justilian had a nasty gash on his forehead. His head had not cleared the camera hatch when he left the plane. After much persuasion, he agreed with me that he would never get to the priest before being captured. Our plan was to go into the mountains and find someone who would help us evade capture.

The first night on the side of the mountain was spent under a shelter of a few logs that someone had improvised. We laid one of the parachutes under us, the other one over us, and huddled close together, trying to keep from freezing to death. In the dark
night we could hear the ice and snow crackle, which, in our fear, sounded like someone sneaking up on us. I thought that the Germans knew exactly where we were hiding. They would certainly come looking before the night was over. Completely exhausted from battling the elements, we had gained only a few hundred yards in our escape effort. I breathed a prayer that God would take care of us, and I had the consolation of knowing that I had a wife, family, and friends back home praying for my safety.

We finally fell asleep from sheer exhaustion. Morning came with the same crackle of the ice around us. I wondered if all crew had gotten out of the plane alive or if they had been killed. Was there some hope of making contact with the Underground? I looked at my nylon escape map and thought we must be at least 700 miles behind the enemy lines. We calculated that we must be near the town of Caporetto, Italy, on the Yugoslavia-Austrian border. Little did I know that we had bailed out almost in the center of much Yugoslavian Partisan activity. Neither did I know that was why the Germans did not come after me and the other flyers who landed on the mountains. It was Partisan Territory! In the chill of that first morning, my mind drifted back home. Geraldine, my wife, would soon be getting the message, a knock at the door with a telegram with the dreaded message from the War Department, "I regret to inform you, your husband is missing in action." Then I thought, "Please, God, don't let my baby girl, Janice Gaye, be raised without a daddy." I knew what a hard time my mother experienced working and trying to feed and clothe my older sister, Mable, and little cousin whom she took to raise when her sister died. My daddy had died suddenly at 29 years of age, when my mother was five months pregnant with me. I did not want my wife to experience the hardships my mother had endured. All these things run through your mind when you are in difficult circumstances.

I heard church bells ringing from a church in the little town

Daughter Gaye with Daddy's picture

The church from which I heard the bells

below us. The sound carried loud and clear from the valley below. It was 6 a.m. It must have been a Catholic church with the bells ringing for Mass. It had been my family's practice to attend Sunday school and church services on Sunday. I had never in all my life heard as lonesome a sound as the church bells calling people to church service. It was there I was made to realize that there was a Higher Power that I could depend on, just for the asking. I prayed to God. I looked at the snow three to six feet deep in places. I was hungry and had a sore throat from eating snow, but I prayed, "Please Lord, I will always give You credit (praise) if somehow You will help us get out of this enemy-occupied land and back to our Air Base." God must have heard and answered my prayer.

    We vowed to continue to try to escape, although I did promise Justilian that if we did not find help by the time we reached the top of the mountain, we would head back toward the town even if it meant capture. The three of us alternated taking the position of lead man to beat down the snow and branches and clear a path for the others. When exhausted, the lead man would drop back, and another take his place. Finally, by mid-afternoon, we discovered a one-room shack with no chimney but smoke coming out from under the eaves. We saw what we thought were footprints in the snow around the building. The silence was frightening, but we decided, friend or foe, it was time to make contact with someone to obtain food and water. Since it was my turn in the lead, I cautiously approached the cabin. Suddenly the door flew open, and two men burst out with high-powered rifles leveled at us. We threw our hands high in the air and shouted, "Americans!" Our would-be assassins grinned, looked at each other, and laid their rifles aside as they approached us with open arms. They were Yugoslavian Partisan Fighters. We had found friends and, at least temporarily, safety.

This first contact with Yugoslavian Partisans was told from their perspective by the armed men who welcomed us to their mountain cabin. Some thirty years after the war, the account of what took place was related by Bogomil Hvala and Janko Kranjc to Edi Šelhaus, whose book gave the views of the two men:

> One evening in January 1945, after four days of tough walking through six feet of snow, my comrade Janko Kranjc and I arrived at our base completely exhausted. We felt we were safe, and no one could reach us in such deep snow.
>
> The next day we heard sounds of engines as we prepared breakfast. This sound always made the Partisans happy, for it meant American bombers were on their way to bomb Hitler's exposed flank. There were many planes in the air. We enjoyed watching these wonderful flocks of steel birds.
>
> It was 1300 hours (1 p.m.) when the flotilla reappeared on its return flight after the mission was completed. The planes had barely disappeared over the horizon when another plane appeared, flying low from the direction of Matajur, toward Krn. We knew that something was wrong with the plane, which was confirmed a moment later as we clearly saw the plane crash into Mount Krn. We turned to look at the sky and saw two little dots that began

to grow, which we confirmed to be parachutes. Two had dropped over Kobarid, two more above Matajur, and three more far below us. Our chief concern was to help the stricken allies before they fell into the hands of the Germans. For those who dropped over Kobarid, there was no hope for rescue as a large German stronghold was located there. Our initial attempts to search for the parachutists were unsuccessful, and further searching was abandoned as night was approaching.

The next morning, we were in for a surprise. We noticed three figures in strange uniforms. We were concerned that they were German ski troops hunting for the flyers. I aimed my machine gun at them and shouted, "Stop, who are you?" There was no reply, so I shouted again, "Hands up!" The closest one [me] lifted his hands and called out, "American!" I then knew that he was not the enemy and shouted "Tito!" in return.

The exchange was followed by a scene that would make any film director happy. The flyer [me] came forward and embraced and kissed me. We invited the frozen and hungry flyers into the stable where we offered them everything that we had (only boiled potatoes). One flyer was Polish [Witkowski], so we could communicate on a limited basis.

The rescued flyers ate and warmed themselves in the stable. These stout fellows had never experienced the conditions in the present

Discussing that fateful day

snow-laden mountains of Slovenia. We set out in the snow, across the mountains, to Matajur to Benecija. With clenched teeth, the flyers heroically proceed through the snow and obstacles in their path. When we finally arrived (I cannot recall if it was Matajur or Strmica), the natives came, after learning they were Americans. Everybody wanted to see and make sure that the persons we brought were really Americans. They were extremely excited. The entire affair was risky as the Germans could have come to this village in the mountains at any moment, and the issue would have had a different ending.

Both Janko and I had to return to our post (spying on the Germans at night in the mountains). We said our goodbyes, and all were thankful.

    The Partisans had helped us to safety through difficult territory. I got their names and hoped that I would see them again one day under happier circumstances.

    The Partisans had taken us to a small town where we ate a meal of Italian food that was the best food I was privileged to eat in the next two months. Many people came to see us as we sat at the dining table. Not able to understand the language was no great barrier. Many people, especially the older people, showed their compassion for us in every way possible. I wanted to return their kindness in some way. I was wearing an inexpensive ring made of aluminum alloy, and I gave it to the lady of the home. She accepted it with a look of kindness that I will never forget. Perhaps the ring would in years to come stir her memory of three cold, hungry flyers she helped in their escape.

    We knew the Germans were near, still searching for us, but the deep snow had hindered them from getting up the mountain. As night approached, we were told to take all our possessions with us to the basement where the cows were sheltered from the winter nights and to leave nothing in the home. If the Germans came and discovered we had been there, the punishment would have been severe, probably even death. We slept on the cold ground against the walls to keep from being stepped on by the cows. We were thankful for a place to sleep out of the severe weather. Many nights to come would find us with no place to sleep except under pine trees, bedding down on branches of pine. We would sleep so close together that the body heat from each other would keep us alive.

A man aroused us early the next morning; we must hurry and get further in the mountains to a home which I will never forget. It was a comfortable house with only a lady dressed in black with a bonnet on her head and a little girl, possibly twelve years old. This lady, Mrs. Amalija Faletič, was like a mother to us, treating us as she would her sons. I never knew, but I thought the sweet and beautiful little girl must have been her granddaughter. Neither Mrs. Faletič nor the girl had any fear of us. We would stay inside the house in the daytime while some man, I know not who, was always on the outside with a high-powered rifle to keep the enemy away.

The snow was very deep and still snowing. I remember taking a corn scoop (big shovel) and digging a path to the barn. This would be our bedroom every night for the next five nights. Again, we slept with the cows. There was not cover for our bodies—we learned to sleep with our flight jacket draped over us. This way we could stay much warmer, rather than wearing the coat at night. Mrs. Faletič had milk and homemade cheese with very little else to feed us. For this we were very thankful. As we left the house at night to face the bitter cold, she would give each of us a large glass of warm milk. One will never know how that milk warmed the whole body. The little girl gave me her name written on a small piece of paper. It may be that one day in time of peace I would return to thank my rescuers.

The snow had stopped falling. I knew that very soon we must resume our travel. The danger was still great of being captured. The word got to us that part of our crew had been captured. We could account for nine men through the Partisans who came to inform us. We thought until much later that Armstrong, the pilot, had gone down with the plane. Armstrong had been captured, and the one missing was the bombardier who had left the plane early and was captured in another city.

I shall never forget the kindness of Mrs. Faletič. She never showed fear or frustration, just kindness and love toward us. I still respect and love her dearly, knowing the price she would have paid if they had found us in her home. These were the most dangerous days for us. The Germans knew we were close by. If she had fear, we never knew it by her actions. She made us feel safe, at least for the time being. We knew once we left there, the bitter cold weather in the Alps Mountains would take its toll, even if we were successful in evading the enemy.

Missing in Action

```
                        WAR DEPARTMENT
                   THE ADJUTANT GENERAL'S OFFICE
IN REPLY REFER TO:      WASHINGTON 25, D. C.
AG 201 Petty, John W.
    PC-N MT0029
                                            9 February 1945


          Mrs. Geraldine T. Petty
          Route #2
          Carthage, Tennessee



     Dear Mrs. Petty:
                    This letter is to confirm my recent telegram in which you were
          regretfully informed that your husband, Staff Sergeant John W. Petty,
          14,153,171, Air Corps, has been reported missing in action since 20
          January 1945 over Italy.

                    I know that added distress is caused by failure to receive more
          information or details. Therefore, I wish to assure you that at any time
          additional information is received it will be transmitted to you without
          delay, and, if in the meantime no additional information is received, I
          will again communicate with you at the expiration of three months. Also,
          it is the policy of the Commanding General of the Army Air Forces upon re-
          ceipt of the "Missing Air Crew Report" to convey to you any details that
          might be contained in that report.

                    The term "missing in action" is used only to indicate that the
          whereabouts or status of an individual is not immediately known. It is
          not intended to convey the impression that the case is closed. I wish to
          emphasize that every effort is exerted continuously to clear up the status
          of our personnel. Under war conditions this is a difficult task as you
          must readily realize. Experience has shown that many persons reported
          missing in action are subsequently reported as prisoners of war, but as
          this information is furnished by countries with which we are at war, the
          War Department is helpless to expedite such reports.

                    The personal effects of an individual missing overseas are held
          by his unit for a period of time and are then sent to the Effects Quarter-
          master, Kansas City, Missouri, for disposition as designated by the soldier.

                    Permit me to extend to you my heartfelt sympathy during this
          period of uncertainty.
                                        Sincerely yours,


                                                J. A. ULIO
                                                Major General
                                            The Adjutant General

   1 Inclosure
        Bulletin of Information
```

Our families notified

OFFICE OF THE GROUP CHAPLAIN
HQ. 460TH BOMB GROUP (H)
APO 520 c/o PM NY

8 March 1945

Mrs. Geraldine T. Petty
Route # 2,
Carthage, Tenn.

Dear Mrs. Petty:

    I am in receipt of your letter regarding your husband S/Sgt John W. Petty, 14153171, who was reported as missing in action on January 20th.

    This mission was over Northern Italy. The plane in which your husband was flying began to lose altitude on its return from the target and to straggle from the formation. It was last seen near the coast over the Austrian-Italian border. No chutes were observed to leave the ship. Up to the present time we have received no additional information regarding the fate of this plane and its crew.

    As a Chaplain I realize how anxious and concerned you must feel. I pray that God will give you comfort and strength to sustain your troubled mind and heart in this difficult time.

    If at any time you feel that I can be of further aid to you please do not hesitate to call upon me.

                             Sincerely,

                             Clayton H. Stowe

                             CLAYTON H. STOWE
                             Chaplain (Capt.) U.S.A.

More information to families

I will have to close for now Mrs. Petty. You try to take everything as easy as possible. I know it will be hard, but I believe Bill would want you to. I feel deep down that he is somewhere behind the German lines waiting to come back. Perhaps you have heard from him. If not I hope you recieve word soon. Until then just try to make the best of everything. I'm sure God is taking care of all the boys.

Sincerely,
Jack

"Somewhere in Italy"
Mar. 5, 1945

Dear Mrs. Petty;

I imagine I should begin this, now, I know I should have written you much sooner, and I've put it off time and time again, and I am still rather reluctant about it because I honestly don't know what to write.

As you already know I can't tell you any thing of what has happened, its against all the rules and regulations and it'd only get myself in a lot of trouble if I tried. Its up to the Headquarters here, and to the War Dept. to tell you, and I'm sure they'll tell you everything, and perhaps more than I can. I am awfully sorry about it, and if there is any way I can help out any at all, I am mo...
me know. I was talking w...

S/Sgt D. Mascih - 35050988
761 Bomb. Sq. 460 Bomb. Gp.
A.P.O. 520 C/o P.M., N.Y., N.Y.

Letters from friends

THE LONG, COLD, 72-DAY WALK BEGINS—
JANUARY 20 TO APRIL 2, 1945

Again, the thought kept coming back to me, "Thank God, we are alive." Many of the crews never had this opportunity to get out of their damaged planes. Some planes with direct hits exploded with no chance for the crews to bail out. Other planes, shot up so bad, would go out of control. It is next to impossible to get out of a spinning or diving plane; the force pins the person inside. If only my wife, mother, sister, and other friends and relatives knew we were still alive.

The long trip from behind the enemy lines continued. We walked at night through the mountains, hiding and sleeping during the day. I noticed we had different guides as we made our way south. These were people who lived in each area where we traveled. They were farmers or ordinary citizens and created little suspicion. They took to the mountains at night to help guide us a few miles through the safest routes. Prearranged, they would meet another man to lead us through the area he knew best. They would go back to their individual homes. We would bed down in some sheltered place and try to get some rest before continuing on our journey in the evening.

After a few days of travel, we found ourselves in the area north of Gorica, in a very heavy campaign. The Germans were trying to wipe out the Partisan activity. We could not continue on the route we had hoped to take, neither could we go back from where we started. We were forced to hide in the same area from one mountain to another.

CONTACT WITH THE BRITISH UNDERGROUND

After what seemed like an endless number of days hiding from the Germans, we finally made contact with the British Underground. I remember a major, a captain, and possibly four or five others with the Underground. They had no special headquarters, but moved about, using wireless communication to reach the 15th Air Force headquarters in southern Italy. They were doing their best to keep our intelligence officers up to date on what was happening behind the line. The Underground personnel stayed with us a very short time, briefing us about the area as much as possible.

One of the most welcome things they gave us was lice powder. We were fighting a battle with the lice crawling on our bodies, especially at night when we got quiet and tried to sleep. As long as we were active, the lice hid in the seams of our clothes; but once we were still, they started crawling about, and we would scratch like a dog with fleas. Precious lice powder—it was wonderful as long as it lasted!

The Underground supplied us with Italian money (lire) to use in the event we had an opportunity to buy food. One of the Partisans volunteered to go into a town nearby to buy something for us to eat. He came back with jars of salty brine fish and salty brine pickles that we could not eat, as hungry as we were. The brine would almost turn our mouths inside out. It was no doubt the best they could do. Food was scarce.

Before the Underground personnel left, they promised to send a message to 15th headquarters that we had made contact with the Yugoslavian Partisans. This was a big morale booster. Maybe they would get the message to our families that we were at least still alive.

Geraldine and Janice Gaye—in my thoughts every day

I learned later that the word did get back to our headquarters in Bari, Italy, but it did not occur to me that the Air Force headquarters would not notify my next of kin that we were alive and safe. I suppose that they did not want to raise false hopes at home, since we were still behind enemy lines.

While our ordeal continued, our friends back at the base were writing letters of consolation to our families, and our families were corresponding with each other in an effort to share the latest bit of information and keep up their morale. Several airmen wrote to my wife, Geraldine, with words of consolation, but they could not reveal, for security reasons, the fact that we had been rescued by Partisans.

One of our buddies who had been sent home with a collapsed lung was able to call my wife from North Carolina and tell her we were alive and relatively safe. Lt. Trebusak, co-pilot, and Sgt. Baumgardner, ball-turret gunner, got back to our base safely in thirty-plus days. They told Jack Jarrett of our safe exit from the plane, and Jack relayed the message to Geraldine by phone and letter when he got home.

Meanwhile, the Germans kept up the pressure on the Partisans. The rifle fire continuing all around us resulted in more downed flyers and others coming together to make a run to get out of this location, if possible. Lt. Roy Cooke, from Delmar, New York, a replacement for Lt. Bill Hockensmith, our navigator, joined our small group. He was hidden by a very nice lady soon after bailing out.

> Yadkinville, N.C.
> July 9, 1946
>
> Dear Mrs. Petty,
>
> I do hope that you will remember me. I think I have written to you a time or two while I was in the army at Macon, Georgia. I was the one that sent the gift for the baby from the boys in P.L.M at Cochran Field.
>
> Just before I was shipped overseas I heard that my dear friend Bill, (your husband) had been killed in action. I left Cochran Field and never found out for sure about it.
>
> I will be looking forward to receiving a letter from you and I sincerely hope it will bring me good news of Bill.
>
> Sincerely,
> Clyde Sizemore

Letters from a friend

List of names of "missing in action" and their family members who were notified. (Five of these men were not on our regular crew. They were replacements for this mission.)

1st Lt. Gerald S. Armstrong	Mrs. Virginia Agnes Armstrong (Wife) 1128 Edgewood Street, NE Warren, Ohio
2nd Lt. Frank B. Trebusak	Mrs. Rose Trebusak (Mother) Rural Free Delivery 1 LaSalle, Illinois
2nd Lt. Leroy J. Cooke *(replacement)*	Mrs. Esther V. Cooke (Mother) 40 Hudson Avenue Delmar, New York
2nd Lt. Frank D'Ambra, Jr. *(replacement)*	Mr. Frank D'Ambra (Father) 1868 Broad Street Cranston, Rhode Island
T/Sgt. Leo J. Lord	Mrs. Lucille F. Lord (Wife) 14 Norfolk Street Fitchburg, Massachusetts
T/Sgt. Thaddeus W. Witkowski	Mrs. Anna Witkowski (Mother) 652 N. Aberdeen Street Chicago, Illinois
S/Sgt. John W. Petty	Mrs. Geraldine T. Petty (Wife) Route 2 Carthage, Tennessee
S/Sgt. Elmo J. Justilian *(replacement)*	Mrs. Rosina Justilian (Mother) Berwick, Louisiana
S/Sgt. Francis L. Baumgardner *(replacement)*	Mrs. Florine Baumgardner (Mother) 83 Frost Parkway Tiffin, Ohio
S/Sgt. James W. Brock *(replacement)*	Mrs. Yvonne R. Brock (Wife) Grant City, Missouri

ALMOST THREE WEEKS WITH NO PROGESS

Almost three weeks had passed without being able to make any progress. The Germans were still trying to pinpoint our location. We moved from place to place in this small area. They seemed to have the area in a circle, slowly making the hiding places smaller.

A British captain, an engineer, came to the mountains to find us. An American sergeant came with him. They had bailed out behind the lines near the Adriatic Sea, in the area of Udine or Triesto, Italy. These men's mission was to draft harbor conditions for future use in case of need to outflank the Germans and Italians with an army land force. One of my greatest regrets was failing to get the names and addresses of these two men. I would have liked so very much to contact the red-headed British captain. He and the sergeant had to be two of the most dedicated men to the Armed Service that I had the opportunity to meet.

The American sergeant, whose parents came from Yugoslavia to live in America many years ago, could speak the Yugoslavian language. This was a valuable service, as he could mix with the natives under an assumed name and get information and other necessary items, like food, to survive. These men had been risking their lives for months hiding in a house near the waterfront on the Adriatic Sea, venturing out when possible to map the harbor.

The captain had completed enough of his work to send back to the Intelligence Department in Bari, Italy. He had received the message that some American flyers were on their way out of enemy territory. He came to us with this highly secret information, sealed in an envelope. Hopefully, all would succeed in our battle to get back safely and hand deliver this information which the Army badly needed to make its plans for a future assault. The only way to get this information from behind the lines to headquarters was by courier. If we would agree, we would be the couriers.

His request was, "In no way let this letter be captured by the enemy." Once before he had attempted to send a part of his map of the harbor by a courier. He later learned that the courier was discovered with information concerning the harbor and the important document was confiscated. The courier's fate was being placed in a dungeon where he starved to death. The warning to us was, "If you see you are going to be captured, destroy the letter, or, as a last resort, eat the letter."

The captain was assisted by a local cobbler who was a double-agent and a patriotic Yugoslavian.

The Germans' rifle fire was getting closer, and now the firing was more constant. The captain and sergeant left hurriedly. It was mid-afternoon—no time to wait for the cover of darkness. We had to leave at once or be killed or captured. We left running for our lives as the Germans approached. We hid in the heavy ground cover of bushes and pines until we dared go back to the place of shelter. To our surprise, the house was occupied by a group of Russian soldiers. Ted Witkowski, Justilian, and I re-entered the one-room building, not knowing what to expect. They must have been stationed in the area to help the Partisans with their underground war.

The next scene is one I shall never forget. There were apparently two young officers commanding the group. They were sitting behind a makeshift table. The thing that had caught our attention was not so much the Russians, who seemed to ignore us, it was the stack of smoked link sausages and loaf of unwrapped French bread. We discussed very quietly some way we hoped to divert their attention and cram a piece of sausage and bread in our flight jackets. We were very hungry, as the only food we had for three weeks was the few eggs acquired from a farmer plus the Partisans would let us eat with them if they had food. They would go out at night and kill a cow, dress and quarter it in the field. Then they would bring the meat into the mountains. This food would last for a few days. One can imagine how good the meat tasted, even without being salted or seasoned.

Yugoslavian Partisans butcher a cow

(Photo by Edi Šelhaus, held by The National Museum of Contemporary History of Slovenia)

A YOUNG FIGHTER'S SOBS NEVER HEARD—CONDEMNED TO BE SHOT—JUNGLE LAW

Back at this one-room house, there was a stir and also uneasiness. Something was happening among the Russian soldiers. Since Ted spoke the Polish language, he was able to understand some Russian language. I was whispering to Ted to try to find out what was wrong. We looked at this commander and his assistant; they could not have been more than twenty years old.

What occurred next was understandable in spite of the language barrier, without understanding the words that were being shouted at the top of the young commander's voice. I still recall with horror two men bursting through the door, holding and pushing another young soldier. The machine guns strapped around the two were pushed into the seized man's ribs. They jerked the young man in front of the commander's table. This man, who appeared to be about twenty years old, was trying to tell the commander something. His sobs were never heard, as the commander never ceased his shouting. Again he was jerked around to be pushed through the door and taken away.

My heart felt pity for this tall, erect, handsome young man. What had he done to deserve such treatment? By this time Ted cornered one of the Russians, getting all the information he could, which was enough to let us know what he did, which would mean only a slap on the wrist—not as much as a court martial—in the U.S. Army. I quickly learned that this was not the U.S.A.

The stark truth came to light. This young, hungry soldier who did not have food, took a piece of the sausage from the commander's table to eat. The Russian explained to Ted that discipline had to be very strict. The verdict, without a trial—"Take the man out and shoot him." He added, this young soldier was brave and had credit for killing thirteen of the enemy. This fact did not seem to make any difference to the commander. He did not want to hear that he was hungry and brave. He had rather condemn him to death than listen. Needless to say, we dismissed the idea of stealing a sausage and bread or anything else of his. If this commander could kill one of his own countrymen, what would he do to a hungry American? There are many such memories embedded in my mind. This one comes back to my memory all too often. I feel sad; it seems like a bad dream.

Feb. 15th

Dear Mrs. Petty,
I received your letter today. I hope and pray that since writing your letter that you have received news of Bill's safety. My husband (Ballard) didn't happen to fly with Armstrong that day and neither did Bill Hockensmith, the navigator. As for the others, I don't know as yet. I received a letter Monday from Armstrong's

More letters of comfort and sadness

A "BLUE" CHRISTMAS FOR THE BRITISH UNDERGROUND AND FOOD AND LETTER FROM HOME STOLEN

The American planes constantly flew over as we tried to make our escape. They were dropping supplies in the mountains for the Partisans. I was told that besides guns and ammunition, the drops contained food and medical supplies. The parachutes were not the white nylon type we used to bail out of a plane, but were made of a highly colored material. The planes came over the mountain at a very low altitude, trying to make their drop where the Partisans were most active. I saw the drops more often as we continued through our escape route.

The Underground heard from home by means of parachute drops. They had been behind the lines many months. They looked forward to the letters and sometime food that we seldom got to them for weeks or months. These were brave groups of men. I was behind the lines, making every effort to get out. These men bailed out at night to risk their lives, knowing they might never return home. In many cases, it would mean sacrificing their own lives for information we desperately needed. The dedicated Underground had its own 1944 Christmas dinner stolen, along with the mail and Christmas greetings from home. The enemy, or certainly not friends, saw the area the drop was made by parachute. Underground members, moving very fast and with thoughts only of good food and messages from home, upon arriving at the sight, found only bits and pieces of mail from their loved ones. Family snapshots torn apart and only remnants of food were left. This brave group of Underground workers had to be braver than ever and still carry on. This had to be one of their bluest Christmases.

The Partisans assigned a man to make the escape from the mountain with us. He was to continue with us until we got out of Yugoslavia. There were two ways of escape. Both had been used many times before. One was to steal our way south to a certain place previously assigned on the Adriatic Seashore. There, under cover of night, a boat of some sort would take us across the Adriatic Sea to southern Italy and safety. The route had been discovered by the Germans and was too risky to take. Many had escaped this way before.

The other route was to continue on through the mountains to a designated place southwest of Zagreb, Yugoslavia. Our destination was a flat river bottom. This had been used for a plane escape. We would take this route for another 150 to 200 miles. I must say I did not know the options until later. We were at the mercy of someone else's decisions.

> Dear Jerry, April 4th
> Since I wrote last I have also had my share of worries. On Monday march 26th I received a letter from the Chaplain of the hospital saying Ballard had been wounded on March 15th while flying his 31st mission over Austria. This was followed by a form card from the hospital, letter from the Chaplain of our church

From Lotus Cooper, wife of bombardier

FIVE GERMAN DESERTERS JOIN US

As our efforts to escape continued, others joined our group. A British plane which was hit a few nights previously lit the whole sky. Two of the plane's crew who were severely burned had somehow survived. They joined the group, trying to evade capture. These men had been blown free of the plane. One of the men had been bandaged by a Partisan medic from his waist to the top of his head. His arms, hands, and head were completely covered, with only an opening for his eyes, nose, and mouth.

Also, five German deserters joined us. They had surrendered to the Partisans with the hope of making their way to southern Italy. They wanted to be held as P.O.W.'s until after the war and then be returned home to their loved ones. These were soldiers, one an officer and the other four enlisted men. They had some things with them, such as first aid equipment that would be of great value to Ted Witkowski within a few nights. They were friendly and willing to share anything they had with us.

Added to the group, which was becoming international, was a young Czechoslovakian. He had escaped from a German labor camp in his native land. He was shot in the chest by rifle fire as he ran for his life. Not being hit in a vital organ, he had survived without medication, walking hundreds of miles to get to the Alps Mountains. Ted Witkowski, who understood the Czech language to some extent, talked with the young man. He wanted to come to America. He had seen American cowboy movies as a child in his home country, and his greatest ambition was to settle out West in the United States and become a cowboy.

It did not seem to matter at this point who one was or from what country he came. We had to keep our spirits up if we were to survive. With the help of God, we made our escape from the "hot spot" of enemy activity.

We were told for the next fifty miles there would be very little Partisan protection. The travel would be dangerous, and we would be in danger of being turned into the Germans, if seen by some natives. Food would be scarce, if nonexistent, for the next week.

We prepared to start our journey about one hour before darkness in what would become the worst night of our escape. The way would be dangerous - putting it mildly. The leader gave orders that we must leave at once. The Czechoslovakian began to object and became so upset that he began to cry. With tears, he said, "Please don't start in daylight, we will be discovered." He vividly remembered the gunshot wound in his chest as he escaped the slave labor camp. Our group started with the Czech objecting. It was not the time to split up; maybe the Yugoslavian leader knew best, but I doubted his judgment. Within my mind things did not seem right.

We could no longer have leaders to come out of their small towns to lead us through their vicinity, to relay us to someone else to go through their well-known area. We were now on our own, with only a compass and an escape map, that I took very good care of. I was never sure this leader knew if he was going in the right direction. He did know where the enemy was located; this was a great help.

We had to descend off the face of a steep mountain as darkness began to fall. From the small town below, I could hear gunfire. Tracer bullets began to make red lights as they screamed through the sky. The firing was coming from behind us, so I was sure we had been discovered. Maybe the Czech was right, and this could be the night we would be captured or killed. Maybe it would have been better had I been captured the day I bailed out of the plane, as I was in good physical condition then. If they captured us now and in our weakened condition, would we be able to survive? Whatever our thoughts, we knew we had to continue, regardless of what our fate would be.

The face of the mountain was so steep, we were able to go only from one bush to another. If we turned loose and failed to grab something to hold to very quickly, the slide in the snow would propel us to a landing against a tree or rocks farther down the hill.

At the bottom of the hill, there was a main highway. We were told it should be crossed hurriedly in hope of not being seen. Immediately across from the highway was a river running parallel to the road. This had to be crossed by wading or swimming. Hopefully, the enemy would not be waiting on the road to capture us. The night was only beginning, and it seemed like an eternity since we started late that afternoon.

We hid on the edge of the roads and listened to hear any noise or movement from the undercover around us. We made a quick dash to get across the road. Again, hiding in the quiet of the night, we took a good look at the cold water with ice and snow on each side. I decided to pull my shoes and socks off and roll my pant legs as high as possible.

Before attempting to cross the river, I looked around trying to find my best friend, Ted Witkowski. I had lost contact with him as we descended the mountain, and this concerned me. I had been raised up like the average boy in the hills of Tennessee, hunting and fishing. I knew something of what it would take to survive. Never had I seen mountains like these in the Cumberland Mountains back home. I knew Ted had little or no experience like this, coming from the heart of Chicago. We had no Army Survival training, which would have at least been a big help to city boys. I had no doubt about Ted's will to continue. The only doubt was, would he be able to keep up with the group?

Off came my shoes and socks. Pant legs rolled as high as possible, my toes dug into the snow as I made my way into the water. It was ice cold: however, no colder than the snow on the bank, I stumbled forward inches at a time, hoping not to fall into a deep hole. Reaching the other side, I was wet only to the waist. As I put on my shoes and socks, my pant legs froze quickly.

The gunfire had increased again, the bright tracer bullets lighting the sky. We had to climb a mountain almost like the one we just descended, if we were to escape. How much longer could I continue? Could I muster enough strength to climb the mountain to what I hoped would be safety for the time being?

I again looked for Ted in the darkness. He was nowhere to be seen. Everyone else seemed to be ahead of me, clinging to vines and trees on their start to another hiding place up this high mountain. I was being left behind; Ted must be in the group up ahead of me, I thought.

I climbed as fast as I could. So many times my feet would slip from beneath me, and I would lose all the gain that I had made. Picking myself up and trying again to catch up with the group seemed hopeless.

Finally, we made it to the mountain top. We began to count heads. The group was propped against trees, trying to recoup enough strength to continue. As I feared, Ted was missing. I searched in the darkness for him. The five German deserters were there, the Czech was there, and Justilian, our camera man and gunner, was there. The other crew members—I cannot remember if there were two or three of the crew who also bailed out—they were there. After a thorough check, one more was missing. The Yugoslavian, who had been appointed to go with us, was also missing.

SMALL HOUSE IN THE MOUNTAINS

The group would wait no longer. I had the choice of going on into the night to find a place of rest, or I could wait there by myself and lose the group completely. We told ourselves, we will stop for the night and hope and pray that nothing drastic had happened to Ted and our Yugo friend. We hoped they would trace our steps and locate us before morning.

Approximately one-half mile away, we could see a distant light in what appeared to be a small house in the mountains. This could be a place to stop, friend or foe, if it did not prove to be a mirage. I do not remember the time—maybe close to midnight. Just as we approached the house, the lights were turned out. We felt there must be some kind of heat in that house, and it seemed to be our one and only chance to keep from freezing to death.

We banged hard on the door. There was no answer or sign of life of any kind. Impatiently, we banged on the door harder, as if to break the door down. The light came on, and the door was opened by a man scared almost to death. The man's wife and little girl were seated on a heated concrete slab, built up like a bed with sides to the floor. One end was enclosed with a door to the other end. A woodburning fire was in a fire box that kept the concrete bed warm. During the cold winter nights in the Alps, this made sleeping very comfortable with a minimum amount of cover.

One can imagine how this family must have felt—in the middle of the night, letting a group in their home. Americans, British, Germans, Yugoslav, and one Czech, all cold, some wet with snow and ice on their clothes. I feel sure they expected the worst. The Slovenians who could speak their language consoled this family. We only wanted to thaw out, and then we would continue our journey, without hurting them in any way.

I shall never forget the scene as we all took a place close to this concrete bed to feel some warmth. The man, woman, and child sat by the bed with their heads bowed, saying over and over again what I believed to be a Catholic prayer. There was a string of prayer beads—I suppose a rosary—which they continually fingered. The little girl's head would tilt to one side as she fell asleep, then she would awaken to say the same prayer over and over. I did not understand the language; however, I am sure God understood every word. There are many things etched or stamped in my memory, and this is one that only death can erase.

FEET FROZEN, TED TAKEN AWAY ON A SLED FOR TREATMENT, THEN RETURNED; GERMAN DESERTERS DISAPPEAR

We heard someone outside trying to get to the door. Our prayers were answered. The Yugoslavian leader and Ted had finally made it. Ted, with his shoes off, held them in his hands, feet bleeding and frozen. The soles of his shoes were slippery, he could not climb the mountain in the snow and ice. He had pulled his shoes off so that he could dig his feet into the snow and not slide back down the mountain. The ice embedded in the snow had played havoc with the bottoms of his feet. Later Ted called it frostbitten; I called the feet frozen.

My estimation of the Yugoslavian leader rose one hundred percent. I knew that he had risked his life to help Ted, my closest friend. It was then I found out the German warrant officer had compassion on Ted, as any caring human being would at a time like this. He had left his German outfit with a roll of gauze, and he used all of that to bandage Ted's feet. What appeared to be a bottle of some type of oil, antiseptic, we thought, was rubbed on his feet prior to their being bandaged.

Before daybreak, we left this humble home without as much as asking for food. This family had helped a cold group of airmen and others stay alive one more night. We bedded down somewhere in another barn or shelter for a short rest. We thanked God that Ted was alive and with us. We knew something must be done to keep down infection in his feet. Two of the Slovenian Underground men arrived with a snow sled. They explained that the only medical care available would be near the area where the fighting was most fierce. This was a sad time for both Ted and me. This would mean for the first time we would be separated. Without shedding a tear, Ted told me just before the men pulled him away on the sled, "Please inform my family when you get out of enemy territory that I will be okay. Tell them not to worry, and I will be back home soon." I have never seen a braver person as they pulled the sled away with Ted bundled up, soon to be treated for severe frostbite and partly frozen feet. Fear gripped me with thoughts of never seeing Ted again.

After about three weeks and many miles in Yugoslavia, the Partisans returned to our group. It was plain to see that Ted's feet were much better; however, they were still so sore he could hardly walk.

I wish I knew more of Ted's treatment. He told me, after returning, that he had been blindfolded soon after leaving our group and was taken to a house to see a doctor. I believe he was moved from house to house in the mountains as the fighting continued to change fronts regularly.

The day that Ted was taken away, I looked around to try to find the five German deserters. None of our men knew what happened. I had learned in this very short time to trust the Germans. They seemed to be a carefree group, especially the youngest one, who appeared to be only a teenager. He would tease by telling me that the enemy was near. He would do this with an expression, grinning, as if to make a run to get away. This was short lived. I feared for the worst. There was no place to hold prisoners behind the lines.

I never saw the Czech again. I hope he got his wish. He deserved it—coming to the States to be a cowboy, as he remembered the American movies with the fast horses, the Indians, and the cowboy that always got his girl.

The going was rough from here until we could get farther southeast into Yugoslavia. Not only was getting food next to impossible, getting water to drink was a problem. The snow was not so deep anymore; however, the ground was still frozen with ice and snow on the mountain trails. I had the only container to carry water to drink. It was the regular Army canteen that I crammed in my pocket just before bailing out of the plane. It was a lifesaver. We did not dare come down out of the mountains to find drinking water. The water was rationed to a swallow each from the canteen until we found a small stream or spring. Our bodies seemed to adjust to lack of food, but the craving, burning inside only got worse from lack of water. On some of the mountain trails, where the sun had shone enough to melt the snow and ice in ox tracks, we could find a little puddle of water. I would lay down on my stomach, blow the trash and manure back enough to sip the water, and wet my mouth and throat. Sgt. Baumgardner, the ball-turret gunner, stayed in the hospital for weeks after returning to our base from eating and drinking contaminated food and water. How I escaped this, I do not know.

I remember some food which was brought to the mountain by a group of ladies. It was about the third day of weeks of travel through highly dangerous areas. The location was somewhere near the Italian and Yugoslavian border. These wonderful ladies were risking their lives to get some food to a group of hungry men. They brought food in pots and pans still warm, and slices of Italian bread, The timing of the feast had to be prearranged, probably mouth to ear with the Secret Underground, as word seemed to travel fast.

Lady Partisans bring food

(Photo by Edi Šelhaus, held by The National Museum of Contemporary History of Slovenia)

Missing in Action

Dear Mrs. Petty,

I thought that I should let you know that after receiving the terrible telegram on Feb. 4th, stating my son, missing since Jan. 20th I have received a card, and letter, dated Feb. 5th on March 12th from my son, from a prisoner of war camp, the ————

Thanking you kindly
Cordially
Frank's mother, Gina D'Ambra
Cranston 5, R.I.

Monday
April 9/45

Dear Mrs Petty —
I recd Your letter today telling me about your husband being on the plane with my husband. I recd a telegram from the War dept Mar 28th telling me my husband was a Prisoner

Sincerely,
Mrs Yvonne Brock
Grant City, Missouri

am glad to know you put your trust in God, atho surely is our only Hope, no matter what happens keep your Faith.

Your sincere friend
Mrs. Florine H. Baumgardner
P.S. Will be praying for you and yours and good news.

Friends continue to write

RATS EAT BREAD FROM MY POCKETS

I questioned the Italian lady who seemed to be the leader. In her broken English and my very limited knowledge of the Italian language, she told me that her husband was prisoner of war of the Americans. He was captured in North Africa, fighting against General George Patton's Army. This dear lady had received a letter from her husband, in an American P.O.W. camp. He wrote that he was getting plenty to eat and not to worry, he would see her when the war was over. This was the lady's way of saying "Thank you, American, for caring for my husband."

We ate hurriedly, thanking the people with all our heart. I looked up to see a group of American bombers flying into Germany to bomb the war factories, oil fields, and supply routes. These people had learned to run and get in ditches for fear of being strafed by gunfire. I stood there looking up with pride as they ran, saying, "Thank you, God. You are still taking care of us." They told us that we had better hide, too. I am sure they were thinking, "If you don't, they will strafe you, not knowing you are Americans." That did make good reasoning; however, the planes were not looking to strafe the enemy, only to bomb their targets and get back to their bases safely.

This lady gave me a loaf of her bread to stuff in my pocket to eat sparingly as we traveled the next few days when food would be very scarce. There would be too much danger of being captured to ask for food. She did not know that in the very next hiding place, my bread would disappear.

We walked until we were exhausted that night, and found a barn in which to bed down with only a few hours until daylight. I do not know why I always lay close to a wall—maybe afraid someone would step on me. Almost too tired to breathe, I pulled my flight jacket off. Soon I felt rats crawling over my body. I raised my arm to hurl a big rat through the air, and I heard a bang as he hit the wall. Too exhausted to stay awake and fight the rats, I fell asleep. The smell of the yeast in the bread had attracted the rats. God only knows why they did not eat me along with the bread. I awoke at daylight to find they had eaten my bread, leaving only a few crumbs.

Meanwhile, back home, my wife was receiving further communications from the Air Force and from friends of mine and their families.

On the bombing mission

A COLD NIGHT AND THE SOUND OF "TAPS"

I vividly recall walking through the mountains, perhaps the next night, and hearing a sound I will never forget. Cold chills ran through my almost frozen body. "Retreat," a military signal for retiring, played on a bugle, sounded loud and clear through the cold crisp night. This sound has to be real. I am still thinking clearly, I can't be hallucinating, or can I? "Taps?" That bugle call means the end of the day, time to retire. It also means the end of a life. I had heard "Taps" played at a military funeral. As we continued into the night, we discovered we had come dangerously close to a prisoner of war detention center where American and other Allies were being held as prisoners of war. If I am fortunate enough to have "Taps" played at the end of my life, it can never be any louder and clearer than it sounded to me on this cold night in the foothills of the Alps. With God's help, I was not going to let "Taps" be the end. I determined to pretend it was a bugle call to get up in the morning and continue fighting these mountains to a safer place.

ADDRESS REPLY TO
COMMANDING GENERAL, ARMY AIR FORCES
WASHINGTON 25, D. C.

ATTENTION: AFPPA - 8   HEADQUARTERS, ARMY AIR FORCES
                                    WASHINGTON

AAF 201 - (11804) Petty, John W.
            14153171

                                                    30 March 1945

Mrs. Geraldine T. Petty
Route Two
Carthage, Tennessee

Dear Mrs. Petty:

    I am writing you with reference to your husband, Staff Sergeant John W. Petty, who was reported by The Adjutant General as missing in action over Italy since 20 January 1945.

    Additional information has been received indicating that Sergeant Petty was the assistant engineer on a B-24 (Liberator) bomber which departed from Italy on a bombardment mission to Rosenheim, Germany on 20 January 1945. The report reveals that your husband's bomber was last seen at about 1:45 p.m., north of Cortina, Italy, while enroute from the target, and it is believed that his plane was lost due to adverse weather conditions. It is regretted that no further information is obtainable in this headquarters relative to the loss of Sergeant Petty's aircraft.

    Believing you may wish to communicate with the families of the others who were in the plane with your husband, I am inclosing a list of these men and the names and addresses of their next of kin.

    Please be assured that a continuing search by land, sea, and air is being made to discover the whereabouts of our missing personnel. As our armies advance over enemy occupied territory, special troops are assigned to this task, and agencies of our government and allies frequently send in details which aid us in bringing additional information to you.

                              Very sincerely,

                              E. A. Bradunas

                              E. A. BRADUNAS
                              Major, Air Corps
                              Chief, Notification Branch
                              Personal Affairs Division
1 Incl.   Assistant Chief of Air Staff, Personnel

GETTING WEAKER

Night after night, as we traveled the foothills of the Alps into Yugoslavia, we wondered how much farther we would have to go until the area would be safe enough for a plane to land and carry us to safety. My body was getting weaker, even though the will to continue on was just as great. My left hip had begun to hurt, and fear gripped me that I might not be able to continue. The only time I remember crying, I sneaked off by myself, with my head in my hands, and the tears flowed freely. After this, I felt better. Maybe it was renewed faith. The pain in my hip seemed to improve.

Soon after this episode, we arrived at a trail that branched into a mountain road, where there was a one-ton, old truck with a flat bed. It was an unusual vehicle, powered by a steam engine. They put wood in a firebox that made the steam for the engine; that made

The foreboding Alps

the truck operate at a very moderate speed. We pulled ourselves on the flat bed of the truck and rode what must have been about twenty miles. It would be hard for anyone to imagine what a great lift that gave us. Our only transportation had been our feet for so long a time. I could not believe what was happening. I will never know if the ride was prearranged by the Partisans or if it was another act of God. The lift gave us new life. Our faith was reinforced that we would arrive at our destination in the near future.

BIBLICAL REFERENCES TO ABRAHAM, LOOKING FOR A CITY

I had always carried a New Testament in my breast pocket on our bombing missions. Maybe I had felt more protected with the Word of God with me. Whatever the reason, the Holy Book was the only thing we had to read during our days and nights spent behind the lines. Looking back, I believe everyone who could read English found a sense of being cared for, even in the darkest time. The subject of faith is discussed in the eleventh chapter of Hebrews—how by faith the prophets of old went forward. The ninth verse says of Abraham "By faith he sojourned in the land of promise, as in a strange country . . ."; the tenth verse, "For he looked for a city which hath foundations, whose builder and maker is God." Another verse in St. John, third chapter, verse sixteen, I had been taught since childhood, "For God so loved the world, that he gave his only begotten son, that whosoever believeth in him should not perish, but have everlasting life." I read the Testament from cover to cover. The others also read it.

The farther we went into Yugoslavia, the less was the danger of being captured. We found barns near farmhouses in the mountains and took the liberty of sleeping in the dry environment rather than on pine branches; that helped in a small way to keep the cold and snowy ground from freezing us.

One cold morning, when I was bedded down in the hay with only my head sticking out, I heard a raving farmer coming. I did not understand a word of his language, but this did not keep him from making his point very clear to me. He had a pitchfork raised in the air coming through the barn door. Since he could see me and the others, it would not do any good to hide under the loose hay. He also was between me and the only door to escape. He cooled off to some degree after which I guess was a cursing that could be heard for a great distance. He finally retreated and we left his barn in a hurry.

Only a few nights after this pitchfork and cursing happened, another incident occurred which I have never forgotten. After walking most of the night and finding a barn that seemed to be away from danger, we found different stalls to bed down for a few hours of sleep. I had just gotten settled behind some hay that was stacked high between me and the door, when I heard a voice from someone coming in my stall. He was speaking the Slovenian language. I did not hear anyone answering him and was afraid to move, even to breathe, for fear of being discovered. This man began to sing and talk some more. I listened and a dog whined, no doubt approving of his master's song. I was exhausted and fell asleep. What happened after that, only the Slovene could tell about. I probably groaned as I fell asleep, sending the man and dog into a hasty flight. When I awoke, there was neither man nor dog to be seen. I wonder until this day what he was doing in the mountains with his dog. Why was he hiding? Maybe he just wanted a rest in the early hours of the morning before daybreak. Strange things happened in the mountains; if a person wanted to get lost for whatever reason, the Alps would be the place to go.

Envelope:
Mrs. L. J. Lord
Fitchburg, Mass.

FITCHBURG
APR 5
5 PM
1945
MASS.

Mrs. Wm. Pitty
Route # 2
Carthage, Tenn.

4-4-45
Wed. 9:00 P.M.

Dear Jerry:

Received your letter from Nashville. Also Gaye's card to Ken. Its cute. Have you heard any more about or from Bill?

Last Thursday I received a War Department wire that Leo is a prisoner of war. I suppose I should be greatly relieved but after thinking he was safe at the base it was

Our families comfort each other.

BOILING CLOTHES TO KILL BODY LICE

A few Partisans arrived to escort us on our journey. Going through a hamlet in the mountains, we passed a house that had a beautiful white dog on a leash in the yard. He was barking fiercely and could be heard for miles. One of the Partisans, with a high-powered rifle, aimed and fired, and the dog dropped dead. As we walked, not more than a mile away, a group of angry men, women, and children overtook us. They seemed to want our Americans more than the Partisans. After much conversation between the natives and Partisans, we were allowed to continue on our way. I did not know what was said; however, there is one thing I am sure of—we almost got lynched, even though we were innocent. Again, these are small things that one does not forget. These heartbroken people wanted revenge, even though the loud barking of this dog could have alerted the enemy that strangers were passing through.

Time had passed—maybe eight or nine weeks—and we had travelled between one hundred and one hundred fifty miles. There was still some distance to go before it would be safe enough to land a plane on some flat area to pick us up. I am sure by now the Yugoslavian Underground was keeping in touch with our Air Force headquarters in Bari, Italy. We had come a long way but were far from out of danger. The Germans still occupied the towns and kept their lifelines open for supplies and ammunition. It was not uncommon to hear rifle fire as we came close to the German forces.

We found a house unoccupied in the mountains. It had a stove that could be used. We would be staying in the first house with a stove since we bailed out. It almost proved to be my downfall. We also found an iron laundry kettle. We boiled water; and taking off all our clothes and placing them in the boiling water, we tried to kill the body lice that we never seemed to be completely rid of. Going back into the house with a fire burning in the stove, we fell asleep on the floor. There was no cover to put under or over us. The wood in the stove burned out soon after we were asleep. We awakened to a bone-chilling cold floor. I felt my head, and I had a burning temperature. Scary thoughts ran through my mind that I was coming down with something and would not be able to go farther with our group. Again, someone from above must have been looking out for me. One of the Partisans had some aspirin. I took the aspirin, my fever broke, and we traveled on.

We were told that in a few more days we would be at a place where planes had landed on a flat field near a river. I am not sure until this day where the place is located, but I was told it would be southwest of Zagreb, Yugoslavia.

About one week before arriving at our destination, we were joined by the British Underground that helped us soon after we bailed out. The English major had been shot and killed as the group escaped from the same mountain from which we made a run to avoid being captured or killed. The captain and his men had been behind our group, making their way to the same place where we were to go. I feel sure they were giving the 15th Air Force headquarters a running account of our flight from the Germans. They had wireless equipment that they had managed to escape with.

The British captain and American tech sergeant also caught up with our group. He took the map of his harbor installation along with a letter to his landlord to deliver himself. I would like so very much to contact these people, if I only knew their names. As I look back now, I realize the exchange of names and addresses could have proved fatal to some people, had the Germans captured this information from individuals.

We were now so near and yet so far away from home. We were soon to learn the hard way that the Germans were still on our trail.

CHIEF WARRANT OFFICER JAMES A. BROOKS

6 April 1945.

Italy.

Dear Mrs. Malone:

I am in receipt of your letter of March 20th, with reference to your son, who is missing. As much as I would like to aid you by giving you some information, it is quite impossible.

The regulations on these matters are quite strict and any information must come through official channels. As you can see, information that I might give could and probably would be hearsay and would only lead to confusion. Unfortunately there is no way for my getting any information that would clear any questions in your mind.

Please forgive my lack of knowledge about your son. By our faith and trust in God we can hope and pray that he will urn home with all the other boys.

Sincerely

James A Brooks

To my mother, Lottie Petty Malone

GERMAN BOMBER BLASTS THE LANDING PLACE FOR OUR DEPARTURE

We arrived at our destination one afternoon with the German dive bombers blasting the location on the river bottom. They knew that planes had landed there previously. I wondered if they had intercepted a message from the Underground that our group was to arrive. They certainly gave us a warm reception.

The Partisans had been expecting this to happen, so they lined out a runway with some kind of material on the opposite side of the river from where the planes had landed for the previous rescue. Shot-down airmen, injured Slovenes, and others had been airlifted to safety. The Germans dropped bombs that created havoc on the wrong side of the river. We learned that it would be too dangerous for our planes to try this rescue again for some time. The Germans would be monitoring this area very closely.

Questions kept coming to my mind—will they return and try another rescue? It is a long way, even farther than when we first started to the Adriatic Sea. There was some talk that this would be our only means of escape. Could we possibly walk another hundred and fifty miles? If we did make it to the sea, would a small boat take the risk of coming in under cover of darkness to rescue us?

We learned that the Partisans were being well supplied by our American airmen at this place. They had parachuted sleeping bags and K-rations of food to this mountain area. It was the first time in about two months for us to have real food and a real bed. Like starved people, we ate the cheese and spam in the K-rations. We loaded our stomachs, which had not been filled in weeks, and it caused diarrhea in a hurry. Getting into my sleeping bag felt so good, until the pain hit again. Having to unzip my sleeping bag and hurry to the woods finally got the best of me. I decided to sit up the balance of the night. Thank God, they did have some toilet tissue with the K-rations.

More flyers whom I had not seen before were coming in our area. Injured Partisans were being brought into the area to be flown out into southern Italy for treatment. It was here I was given a passport. That meant they had hopes of flying us out of Yugoslavia.

On the seventh day after arriving, we received the good news that two American planes would land within an hour to pick up their

Loading injured on plane for flight out

(Photo by Edi Šelhaus, held by The National Museum of Contemporary History of Slovenia)

cargo of injured people and others and then take off almost as soon as they landed. It was a beautiful sight to see these planes lowering their landing gears on the plot of ground beside a river. These planes, I was told, would be flown by South African pilots. High in the sky, we could see three British Spit-Fire Fighters flying escort and cover for the two planes. The German planes would have a fight in the sky if they tried to bomb or strafe the planes.

Again, without experiencing something similar to this, a person cannot imagine just how thankful one can be, knowing that within two hours or less of flight time we could be back to safety in Bari, Italy, our 15th Air Force headquarters.

Hurrying to get aboard the plane, we waved to our Partisan friends left behind. We had a bumpy ride before becoming airborne. As the plane rose in the sky, I looked down to see the tough trail we were leaving behind. I then looked up to thank God for all the people involved in our rescue. So many people had so unselfishly risked their lives that others could survive and go back to their bomb groups, hospitals, and in time, home to their loved ones.

Passport to leave Yugoslavia

Passport to freedom

ONE OF THE HAPPIEST DAYS OF MY LIFE

When we landed in Bari, Italy, I kissed the ground. It was so nice to be back to friendly territory. The first order of business was to be taken to a building with a huge room for taking a shower. They took all our clothes and destroyed them. After the bath and before giving us different clothes, they sprayed us with a disinfectant powder to kill any remaining lice. All this was not too bad. I knew better things were coming.

From here, we were taken to headquarters. The Intelligence Department interrogated us, starting from the bail-out until we were flown from behind the lines. The information they got from returned flyers would help prepare another flyer to make it home.

I wanted to know if I could inform my wife and family that I was safe and back at Air Force headquarters. I was told this was not allowed. The message of our return would have to go through proper channels to the War Department in Washington. The War Department would notify the next of kin of our safe return to duty. I knew this would take days. I wanted very much to get the information to my family that I was alive, not injured, and would go to the Army Hospital for a thorough physical check-up.

The reason for a person not to call home at once was to avoid confusion. The next of kin would receive the telegram from the returned airman and, not being sure of the circumstance of the message, would contact the War Department in Washington. The War Department would not have received the message of the flyers being returned to duty, since it would take days to process and relay the news through proper Air Force channels, due to the red tape involved. The War Department would notify the next of kin that the husband or son was still "Missing In Action." This could cause more confusion and heartache than if the family had not received the message for a few more days.

I must confess I broke Army regulations. I was told by a compassionate officer in the Communications Department that I would not be charged with disobeying orders if I wanted to send a message by telegram. This could not be a personal message; the words I could use would be enough to serve the purpose that I was well and safe.

I spent one night in the base hospital in Bari, Italy. I was discharged the next day to return to the 460th Bombardment Group located in Spinazzola, Italy.

I wanted to know if members of our crew who were not flying with us were still alive and making missions. I had a reunion with Cooper, our bombardier, who had been injured in the face and arm from anti-aircraft bursting shell. He had received the Silver Star medal for bravery. The navigator on the crew he was flying with was injured very badly. Mort Cooper, a brave man, ignored his own injuries to keep the injured navigator on oxygen.

Duane Mascik, tail gunner; Kelly Mitchell, the ball turret gunner; Jay Wilson, waist gunner, who had been grounded because of air sickness, were all there to greet us. We had a great reunion, with much to tell each other. Jack Jarrett, waist gunner, had been returned to the States because of a collapsed lung. I did not get to see Bill Hockensmith, our navigator, on my return. The information was that he was well and still flying as lead navigator for our group.

Frank Trebusak, the co-pilot, who had bailed out with us, had gotten from behind enemy lines much quicker than the group with whom I came out. Frank's ancestors came from the Slovenian part of Yugoslavia, and he could speak their language. This helped him and the tail gunner, Baumgardner, to get through to a place from where he could be flown out of enemy territory much quicker than our group. Sgt. Baumgardner, the replacement for Clinton K. Mitchell, was still in the hospital due to a stomach virus from eating contaminated food somewhere behind the lines. I was told that he had been in the hospital for weeks and was still confined. I have not heard any word from him since that time.

Ted Witkowski, our radio operator, was placed in the hospital, where he would remain for many weeks due to the condition of his feet from being frozen and frostbitten.

There was definitely a sadness as I returned to our six-man tent on the base. We had gone to a farmer's straw stack and acquired enough straw for our beds. As I looked down on that bunk, the straw-filled mattress cover looked like the most expensive perfect-sleeper mattress one could imagine. I looked again at the empty bunks. Leo Lord, our engineer, was gone, a prisoner of war; Ted Witkowski in the hospital; Jack Jarrett returned to the States because of a collapsed lung. Then my mind went back to the bail-out and pilot Jerry Armstrong, staying with the plane, fighting the controls to keep the plane upright until the last man exited the plane. He almost waited too long. I was told that he was so close to the ground that when his chute opened, swinging him to the right or left and on the back swing, he hit the side of the mountain with a bang. Jerry was rescued by a family but was free only a few hours before the Germans came to take him away.

Again, standing in the tent at the base with the empty beds, I thanked God that we were all still alive. Then an orderly came with a message that Colonel Price, our commanding officer of the 460th Bombardment Group, was expecting me to come to headquarters and have dinner with him.

Before I left the tent, my friends told me of gathering my personal things, such as pictures of my wife and baby, Janice Gaye, and whatever I had kept around my bed to have a little home atmosphere, were sent to our 761st supply house. They had been kept there for sixty days. After the sixty days, these items would be placed in a box labeled "Missing In Action," and returned to my wife. By this time, my things had already been sent to 15th headquarters.

The supply officer sent to Bari, fifty miles away, to retrieve these items so that I could bring them home personally.

The invitation from Colonel Price was greatly appreciated. We spent some time reminiscing about the flight of January 20 to Linz, Austria. Some of the topics we talked about were how the sky was black with bursting shells from anti-aircraft guns. Another item that we could not forget was the severely cold weather. To the best of my memory, he told me that twenty-plus airmen returned with frostbitten hands and feet. I remember my hands got so cold that my knuckles were swollen for days.

I had been flying as assistant engineer, my engineer rating having resulted from working as a mechanic on planes the first year I was in service at Cochran Field in Macon, Georgia. I was awarded a Certificate of Valor in recognition of courageous service in aerial combat by Major General Nathan Twining, Commander of the 15th Air Force. It was also signed by Col. John Price, Commander, 460th Bombardment Group, and Brig. General Acheson, Commander, 55th Bombardment Wing.

I spent only a few days at the base in Spinazzola, Italy, where I received my promotion from Staff to Tech Sergeant and first Engineer rating.

I arrived in Naples, Italy on April 18, 1945, there to await an Army flight back to the States. While I was in Naples, news came that President Franklin D. Roosevelt had died. The shock of his death was very apparent, not only to the American servicemen but to the Allies as well. The big question seemed to be, can someone take President Roosevelt's place as our leader?

One other thing I remembered was a one-man show put on by Red Skelton. This was a man who gave his all to cheer up the men overseas.

CERTIFICATE OF VALOR

15

AWARDS AND RECOGNITIONS:
Air Medal - 1 OLC
LSME Ribbon - 2 Battle Stars

SPECIAL ACHIEVEMENTS:
Engineer Gunner
17 Sorties over enemy territory.

JOHN W. PETTY
TECHNICAL SERGEANT

Major General Nathan F. Twining, Commanding Fifteenth Air Force has directed that this certificate be presented you

IN RECOGNITION OF COURAGEOUS SERVICE

AERIAL COMBAT

CAMPAIGNS:
Rome-Arno Campaign
Southern France Campaign

JOHN M. PRICE
Col., Air Corps,
460th Bombardment
Group, Commanding

ROGER W. ACHESON
Brig. General, USA, Commanding
55th Bombardment Wing

```
                    ** EXTRACT **
                                                    Section
Awards of Air Medal and/or Oak Leaf Cluster for the Air Medal.......... 1

            761st Bombardment Squadron, 460th Bombardment Group (H)

SECTION 1   AWARDS OF THE AIR MEDAL AND/OR OAK LEAF CLUSTER FOR THE AIR MEDAL

         Under the provisions of AR 600-45, as amended, and pursuant to auth-
ority contained in Circular No. 89, MATOUSA, 30 July 1944, The Air Medal
and/or Oak Leaf Cluster for the Air Medal, in the categories as listed is
awarded the following named personnel Air Corps, Army of the United States,
residence as indicated, for meritorious achievement in aerial flight while
participating in sustained operational activities against the enemy between the
dates as indicated, and/or for meritorious achievement in aerial flight while
performing an act of merit as indicated.

                            AIR MEDAL

JOHN W. PETTY, 14153171, Sergeant, Carthedge, Tennessee.  17 September to
4 October 1944.

                    _____  OAK LEAF CLUSTER (BRONZE)

                 By command of Major General TWINING:
```

WESTERN UNION

12.
Fitchburg, Mass. 12.1 PM 25

T. Sgt & Mrs Wm Petty
Carthage, Tenn

Received letter from Leo expect him home any day both well love.

Lucile.

WESTERN UNION

NL.Pd
Venice, Utah.16

Mrs. Wm Petty
Carthage, Tenn.

Ballard is to start home soon he said Bill might beat him home. Are you as excited as I am. Will try and write to nite,

Lotus.

FROM S/Sgt. Jack Jarrett
ASN 14162132
U.S. Army Air

Have heard the good news!! and I'm really glad. Told you he would turn up safe and sound! I am traveling now but will write soon. Jack

To Mrs. J. W. Petty
Route 2
Carthage, Tenn.

Coming home

HOME AT LAST

I left Naples on April 18, 1945, arrived in Casablanca, Africa, to spend four days before continuing home on a C-54 transport plane. First stop was the Azores, then on to Bermuda, from there arriving in Miami at 2:30 p.m., April 23, 1945. From there I was given a 60-day leave to come home to be with my loved ones.

I was happy to be home with Geraldine, Gaye, and my friends, but I was still a little unsettled. I was asked many questions about my experience behind enemy lines, but I had signed a document promising secrecy. It stated:

> I will not reveal any information concerning my escape or evasion from capture, by those that helped me, the method of escape, the route I took, or any other facts concerning my experience while behind enemy lines. Disclosure to anyone except an Officer designated by the Commanding General of the Theater of Operations will make me liable to disciplinary action.

I would be liable to disciplinary action, carrying a heavy penalty, if I revealed this information to any unauthorized person. I was not to give an account of my experience in books, newspapers, periodicals, in broadcasts or lectures. Discovery of escape information would put the lives of the ones who helped in jeopardy and would prevent escaping or evading capture by others.

After sixty days at home, I reported back to the Air Force headquarters in Miami, Florida, and given the same status as an ex-prisoner of war. I was allowed to bring Geraldine to Miami Beach for two weeks of relaxation and fun before being reassigned for duty.

Leaving Miami, I reported to Fort McPherson in Atlanta, Georgia, where I was informed of a "point system" based on time spent in the Armed Services, time in Combat overseas, and other factors. I learned I had built enough points to get a discharge back into civilian life if I so chose.

If my decision was to continue in the Air Force, I could be assigned to an Air Base of my choice and the opportunity to apply for officer training to become a commissioned officer. This was offered to show appreciation for the time spent behind enemy lines. I expressed my gratitude and requested that I be separated from the Service to return home. A few days later I was given an Honorable Discharge to return to my family in Carthage, Tennessee.

It was so good to be back. Again, I was made to realize how God had answered not only my prayers but those of my loved ones too. My memory had to go back only a short time to realize many would not be coming back: the planes I saw blow up in a ball of fire from direct hits or the damage to other planes that went out of control without the crew having a chance to bail out. This was the price that many paid. Lest we forget, this is the price that was paid for your freedom and mine. We are the fortunate. Many of the "missing in action" did not have the opportunity to return as I did.

Since our nation was formed, men, women and children have suffered, and many have given their lives in battle that you and I can have and appreciate the "Land of the Free," one nation, under God, with liberty and justice for all.

May God ever keep it this way.

```
ENLISTED RECORD AND REPORT OF SEPARATION
            HONORABLE DISCHARGE
```

1. LAST NAME - FIRST NAME - MIDDLE INITIAL	2. ARMY SERIAL NO.	3. GRADE	4. ARM OR SERVICE	5. COMPONENT
Petty John W	14 153 171	T Sgt	AC	AUS
6. ORGANIZATION	7. DATE OF SEPARATION	8. PLACE OF SEPARATION		
1020th Army Air Forces Base Unit	21 Jul 45	Separation Center Fort McPherson Ga		
9. PERMANENT ADDRESS FOR MAILING PURPOSES	10. DATE OF BIRTH	11. PLACE OF BIRTH		
Rt 2 Carthage Tenn	22 Mar 18	Carthage Tenn		
12. ADDRESS FROM WHICH EMPLOYMENT WILL BE SOUGHT	13. COLOR EYES	14. COLOR HAIR	15. HEIGHT	16. WEIGHT	17. NO. DEPEND.
See 9	Brown	Brown	5'11"	149 LBS.	2
18. RACE: WHITE X	19. MARITAL STATUS: SINGLE X	20. U.S. CITIZEN: YES X	21. CIVILIAN OCCUPATION AND NO. Manager Retail Store 0-72.91

```
              MILITARY HISTORY
```

22. DATE OF INDUCTION	23. DATE OF ENLISTMENT	24. DATE OF ENTRY INTO ACTIVE SERVICE	25. PLACE OF ENTRY INTO SERVICE
	11 Nov 42	11 Nov 42	Nashville Tenn
26. REGISTERED: YES X	27. LOCAL S.S. BOARD NO. Not Available	28. COUNTY AND STATE	29. HOME ADDRESS AT TIME OF ENTRY INTO SERVICE See 9

30. MILITARY OCCUPATIONAL SPECIALTY AND NO.
Aerial Engineer-Gunner   748

31. MILITARY QUALIFICATION AND DATE
MM Pistol   Aviation Badge

32. BATTLES AND CAMPAIGNS
Rhineland   Central Europe
Rome-Arno   Northern Apennines   Po Valley   Air Combat Balkans   Southern France

33. DECORATIONS AND CITATIONS
Air Medal with 1 Oak Leaf Cluster   Good Conduct Medal
European African Middle Eastern Theater Ribbon with 7 Bronze Stars

34. WOUNDS RECEIVED IN ACTION
None

35. LATEST IMMUNIZATION DATES
SMALLPOX 28 May 44   TYPHOID 16 Sep 44   TETANUS 3 Feb 44   OTHER

36. SERVICE OUTSIDE CONTINENTAL U.S. AND RETURN

DATE OF DEPARTURE	DESTINATION	DATE OF ARRIVAL
11 Aug 44	European Theater	22 Aug 44
18 Apr 45	United States	23 Apr 45

37. TOTAL LENGTH OF SERVICE
CONTINENTAL SERVICE: 1 YEAR 11 MONTHS 29 DAYS
FOREIGN SERVICE: 0 YEARS 8 MONTHS 12 DAYS

38. HIGHEST GRADE HELD: T Sgt

39. PRIOR SERVICE
None

40. REASON AND AUTHORITY FOR SEPARATION
Convenience of the Government RR1-1 (Demobilization) AR 615-365 15 Dec 44

41. SERVICE SCHOOLS ATTENDED
AAF Flexible Gunnery 6 Weeks 1944 Grad

42. EDUCATION (Years): Grammar 8   High School 0   College 0

```
              PAY DATA
```

43. LONGEVITY FOR PAY PURPOSES: 2 YEARS 8 MONTHS 11 DAYS
44. MUSTERING OUT PAY: TOTAL $300   THIS PAYMENT $100
45. SOLDIER DEPOSITS:
46. TRAVEL PAY: $14.40
47. TOTAL AMOUNT: $187.10   NAME OF DISBURSING OFFICER: JACK GOLDSMITH Capt FD

```
           INSURANCE NOTICE
```

48. KIND OF INSURANCE: Nat. Serv. X
49. HOW PAID: Allotment X
50. EFFECTIVE DATE OF ALLOTMENT DISCONTINUANCE: 30 Jun 45
51. DATE OF NEXT PREMIUM DUE: 31 Jul 45
52. PREMIUM DUE EACH MONTH: $6.70
53. INTENTION OF VETERAN TO: Continue X

55. REMARKS
Lapel Button Issued

56. SIGNATURE OF PERSON BEING SEPARATED
John W. Petty

Asst PERSONNEL OFFICER
DAVID GOLDBERG
1st Lt AUS
David Goldberg

WD AGO FORM 53-55
1 November 1944

Record and report of separation

Army of the United States

Honorable Discharge

This is to certify that

JOHN W PETTY 14 153 171 Technical Sergeant

1020th Army Air Forces Base Unit

Army of the United States

is hereby Honorably Discharged from the military service of the United States of America.

This certificate is awarded as a testimonial of Honest and Faithful Service to this country.

Given at SEPARATION CENTER
Fort McPherson Georgia

Date 21 July 1945

CONWAY BORUFF
Major AUS

My discharge paper

THE RETURN

My joy over leaving Yugoslavia was so great that for a long time I did not seriously consider returning. Yet thoughts of gratitude increased over the years until I felt compelled to try to personally express appreciation to the brave Partisans who, at great risk, had helped us.

In 1969, Geraldine and I visited Kobarid and found Mrs. Amalija Faletič, the lady who hid me and two other crew members from the Germans after we bailed out. She was 88 years old then and could remember very well about letting us stay with her. We gave her a gift, and mailed things back to her later, but she would only say, "The things I did, I never did to be repaid. I did them with compassion and goodness in my heart." This lady would probably have been killed if the Germans had found us there.

The trip was one we shall never forget. After an arduous trip, which included crossing the Yugoslavian border, we made our perilous way over a narrow road to a point near the Faletič home. Things were amazingly the same as I had remembered them. The barn where I slept with my two buddies remained unchanged. Someone brought Mrs. Faletič to the front yard of her home. She looked at me, long and silently. I tried to tell her who I was. The cab driver who had driven us there tried to help with communication. Finally, she understood and embraced me, remembering the time years before when she had taken us into her home. The reunion was charged with emotion.

After our return in 1969, we began to make plans to visit Kobarid again. Thus, on August 14, 1976, Geraldine and I went to

Missing in Action 75

After 24 years, I met Mrs. Faletič again. At age 88, she was still very active.

Yugoslavia to visit our friends we had visited in 1969. This time, the pilot of our B-24 bomber, Gerald Armstrong, and his wife, Jenny, made the trip with us.

I had written Mr. Edi Šelhaus, the editor of a newspaper in Ljubljana, Yugoslavia, that we planned a visit to their city and hoped to return to the village of Kobarid to visit the friends who helped us so much during World War II. Kobarid is about 100 miles from Ljubljana and is near the Italian, Yugoslavian, and Austrian borders in the Alps Mountains. Before the war, the town was known as Caporetto.

On August 23, we left Ljubljana with Edi Šelhaus to go to Kobarid. When we arrived, we were treated with royalty by the Yugoslavian people. They had done a lot of work to get in touch with the people who had helped us and to let them know that we were coming.

Everyone welcomed us. They had gathered information about our bail out and Mr. Šelhaus had written a book about it. Obviously, all this captured our intense interest.

Mr. Šelhaus and the Partisans had arranged our trip. We left the Hotel Lev in Ljubljana very early in the morning and returned late that night, but for one day we accomplished a lot.

With Mrs. Faletič's daughter-in-law in front of the barn where we were sheltered

Edelweiss, the beautiful flower of the Alps

One of the people I wanted to see most was Mrs. Faletič, whom we visited in 1969. We were too late. She had died the year before at the age of 95. Her son and daughter-in-law still lived in the house where we stayed with her. Not much had changed about the house or the barn where we slept with the cows.

I also wanted to visit with the two Partisans whom we contacted soon after we bailed out of the plane. These men were an answer to an earnest prayer we had prayed—that God would lead us in the right direction. Any other direction would have led us into German hands, and we would have been captured. We had climbed to the top of this snowy mountain where these two men had welcomed us and put us on the right trail. We will always be grateful to these men. They were Bogomil Hvala and Janko Kranjc.

We first visited the Bogomil Hvala family in Tolmin. Bogomil and I talked over old times. The family made us feel welcome, serving cookies and coffee. They had a son in his last year of college and a daughter who had finished college and taught in a a school in Ljubljana. She accompanied us on the rest of the trip. She spoke English very well and was a big help to us.

While in Tolmin, we went into the main part of town and met with more of the Partisans. We were introduced to the president and secretary of the Partisans. These men gave us a big welcome. We also met Darko Ohojak, who had rescued the co-pilot. He went with us to Kobarid.

When we got into Kobarid, where we had bailed out, there were lots of people to welcome us. While the pilot, Gerald Armstrong, and his wife visited the jail where he had been kept as prisoner, Geraldine and I visited with Janko Kranjc and his family. Ivan (Janko's Partisan name) and his family were working in their hay field at the foot of a beautiful mountain.

I will ever be grateful to these two men, Janko and Bogomil, for helping us to get out of the area where the plane crashed.

Darko Ohojak, who rescued the co-pilot from the Germans, along with his son, gave me a piece of the shroud line to my parachute. His wife had saved it all these years.

There is so much I would like to tell about these kind people who treated us so nicely. The Partisans furnished a car and driver and served us a nice meal. Dusan Mencin, a young Yugoslavian attorney who spoke English, was our driver. Mr. Šelhaus had a reporter, a Mr. Ogarev, who went with us all day. He wrote a full page about our trip, and it appeared in the Yugoslavia newspaper. Mr. Šelhaus also spent most of the night developing photographs for us to bring home. He had them at the hotel early the next morning.

These are some of the people I was with during the 72 days behind enemy lines. They walked approximately 200 miles with us at night through the mountains, so that we could be flown out of enemy territory.

There is absolutely no adequate way to express the depth of my gratitude and appreciation.

Viewing the mountain where we were rescued 31 years previously

Reunion with Janko

Geraldine and Bill with Mrs. Faletič's daughter-in-law

Reunion with Bogomil Hvala and daughter, Nevenka

(Photo by Edi Šelhaus, held by The National Museum of Contemporary History of Slovenia)

Our driver, Dusan Mencin, and Geraldine

Jerry Armstrong and Bill view the wing of their crashed plane. It was being used for a barn door. A small part of the wing has been added to the USAF Museum collection at Dayton, Ohio.

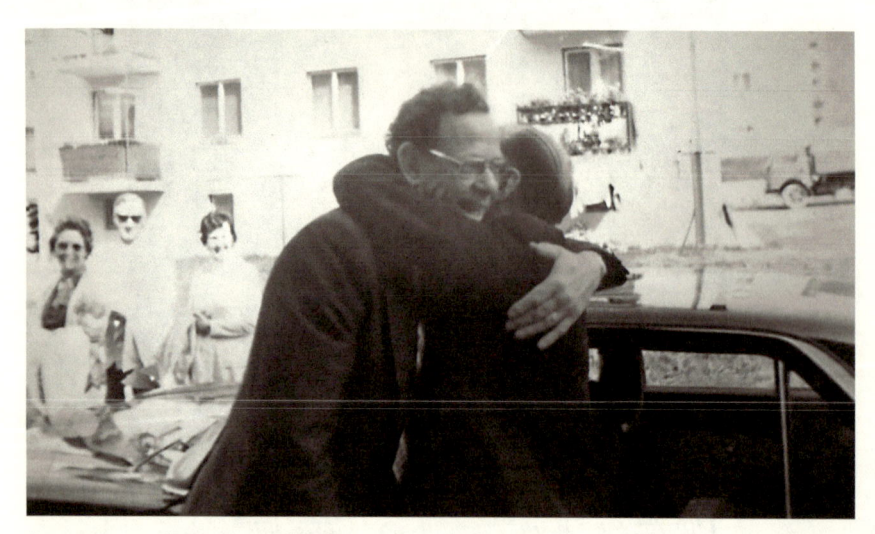

Reunion with Bogomil Hvala

Geraldine, Nevenka, and Bogomil Hvala with reporter Andrej Pagon Ogarev

Friends at Kobarid turn out to greet us.

APPENDIX

God is good—and His goodness has been demonstrated in innumerable ways throughout the years. As mentioned previously, Geraldine never gave up hope that I would return. Her faith was so strong that each day she wrote me a letter, even though she knew it could not be delivered. Her faith became a reality when I was able to return to her and our daughter.

God has blessed our family, for which Geraldine and I are grateful. In addition to our first daughter, Gaye, another daughter, Joye, was born soon after the war. Gaye has one son, Tony Hawks, a graduate of University of Tennessee with a Civil Engineer degree. He lives in Atlanta. Their daughter, Penny, a graduate of Northern Michigan University, has her degree in Computer Science and Accounting. Gaye is supervisor with the City Schools in Lebanon, Tennessee. Penny is married to Randy Maberry, a pilot with American Airlines. Randy and Penny have two children, Brandon and Alicia.

Joye has two daughters, Michelle Key, a graduate of University of Richmond. She is a technical writer and is completing her master's degree at Vanderbilt University. Rebecca, the youngest daughter, is a Senior at Germantown High School. She is an honor student and a member of the soccer team. Joye is a registered nurse and renal program administrator with the University Physicians Foundation in Memphis. She lives in Germantown, Tennessee.

This section may be of interest to you as a reader, but it is included primarily for my family who encouraged me to write this book for posterity.

Bill and Geraldine Petty

> Wednesday — Feb. 7, 1945
>
> Honey, I hadn't heard from you in over a week until wed. morning — Rec. the letter written the 19th. A letter from Mrs. Witkowski came saying Ted was missing, so naturally I was all torn up about you but everyone had consoled me that you were all right when Jake & Anne came with the telegram, saying you had been missing since Jan. 20, in Italy. Needless to say how I felt, for you know how much I love you. Little Faye knew something was wrong & they could hardly quite her. I had been worried about you but kept praying you were all right. Myrtle, Mrs. Hallie, Ila & Clara Lee were here & then Jake & Anne came with the message. Bro. Duesver came in just a few minutes, he prayed such a pretty prayer & Honey, so many are praying & too, God has never failed you & me & I can't believe he will this time. He gave me strength to hold up & I just feel you are somewhere praying for me too. Mable & Ernest came, also Mary, Oma Dale, Lorene & Charles,

Letters written—never mailed—no mail call behind enemy lines

Blalys & Katherine Anne, Mrs. Hunter, Bitsy, Sissie, that nite, Elsie, Shack & kids, Mattie & Parland, & Bitsy & Jeff, Henry, & Eula

Thursday – Jan. 8, 1945.
Went to Mrs. Hattie's & called Mrs. Wilkinson, Ginger had gotten her telegram Sunday. I can't remember who all came that day as to-day is Saturday that I'm writing this, some were: Mrs. Fisher & Fay, Mrs. Bessie Bibbs, Anne, Cousin Minnie Thompson, I just can't remember who else.

Friday – Feb. 9, 1945
That morning Mrs. Frances Bibbs came, Mrs. Barrett, Anne, Mary. After dinner, Rebecca came, Ruth McKinney, Gordon, & Anne. The first nite Eula slept in the room with us but for the last two nites no one has. We are carrying on as usual, you wouldn't believe it was me, just by God's help & your prayers & everyone else's, my strength is lasting. I've been praying for God to give me faith enough to never doubt a minute but what you are all right & I've felt so much better about you that I believe He is giving it to me.

Letters written daily for 72 days—no P.O. Box to send them to

Missing in Action

Daughter Gaye Petty Hawks

Granddaughter Penny with husband Randy Maberry, Brandon and Alicia

Grandson Tony Hawks

Missing in Action

Daughter Joye Petty Key

Granddaughters Rebecca and Michelle Key

Made in the USA
Columbia, SC
19 August 2025